COMMENTS ABOUT ~~LEADER~~SHIP IQ

Through Leadership IQ's webinars I learned more in one hour than I have in many other 8 hour programs. The concepts are so practical that I begin implementing the learning the same day.
Paul Crampton, Ph.D., Director, Leadership Development, White Memorial Medical Center

The information presented was outstanding. Mark is inspirational and kept everyone's interest during the presentations. We have implemented his 'Five Deadly Sins of Teams' within our organization and have seen a marked improvement in team meetings, participation and outcomes.
Jack Kules, Director, Corporate Training & Development, KV Pharmaceutical

Mark Murphy is an incredible Teacher. His programs are very easy to follow and to comprehend. Why are they so beneficial and worth the money? Because they are REALISTIC ! They are very easily applied to today's business environment.
Jeff Markowicz, General Manager Skyline Club, Indianapolis

After participating in 'The Five Deadly Sins of Retention', I was hooked. The information presented was timely, relevant and incorporated practical ideas to take away and implement. It is refreshing to see training material that takes tested and proven concepts and applies them to 'real world' problems. Thank you!
Laurie J. Raimondi, Director of Human Resources, American Safety Insurance

These programs combine the best of quality, content, time efficiency, convenience and cost. This is a rare combination of incredible value.
Frank G. Mikan, President, The HDH Group, Inc.

As one who has been in management for 35 years, I thought there was little I didn't know about the pitfalls of hiring. After taking 'The 5 Deadly Sins of Hiring,' I revamped my entire hiring process from beginning to end to make sure I never have another 'mismatch.' Great information in a concise, well-organized package.
Rita Zwern, Manager, State Programs Business Line, Kaiser Permanente

We found that the webinars that we viewed were leading edge material. They have provided us with a chance to measure and improve our existing practices in a very short space of time. I recommend Leadership IQ to any entity engaged in HR activity from hiring to Board level participation.
Eric L Kudaka, HR Director, Wasaya Airways LP

The subjects pertain to real issues facing all organizations today, and the presentations are practical with specific tools to use, not just theory.
Clare Carmichael, VP Human Resources, Eyetech Pharmaceuticals, Inc.

The time to participate in one of the Leadership IQ courses is a worthwhile investment. They provide practical, actionable information that can directly impact leaders as soon as they leave the session. Thank you!
Deb Wells, Operations Analysis Manager, SUPERVALU

I have been an HR executive for 15 years and have had the opportunity to deliver a variety of leadership training programs. I find the selection and quality to be outstanding with Leadership IQ. There are many out there to choose from but Leadership IQ has made it simple for me by identifying the key skills for development of top leaders and with top-notch materials.
Susan Conti, Director of HR, Spectrum Brands

The Deadly Sins of Employee Retention

Leadership IQ Press

Copyright © 2005 Mark Murphy and Andrea Burgio-Murphy

ISBN: 1-4196-2325-7

Library of Congress Control Number: 2005911231

To order additional copies, please contact us.
Leadership IQ Press
www.leadershipiq.com
800-814-7859
orders@leadershipiq.com

The Deadly Sins of Employee Retention

Mark Murphy
Andrea Burgio-Murphy

For Isabella

TABLE OF CONTENTS

INTRODUCTION

A recent Leadership IQ study found that 24% of employees are actively seeking other jobs (they're submitting resumes and applications, and going on interviews). An additional 32% are passively looking (they're browsing job boards and their resumes may be posted).

As if those numbers weren't bad enough, 47% of **high performers** are actively seeking other jobs while an additional 44% are passively looking. Losing an employee is bad enough. But losing a high performer can be devastating.

Every organization wants to retain their employees, especially their best employees. And most organizations are exerting extra effort to keep them.

But most organizations, and their leaders, are making serious mistakes. We've studied more than 100,000 leaders and we've identified the Deadly Sins of Employee Retention. These are the 5 mistakes that can destroy an organization's retention efforts. The bad news is that they're so harmful. The good news is that they're easily corrected.

This book will challenge some of the most entrenched and misguided beliefs about employee retention. We'll show you how to avoid the Deadly Sins of Employee Retention and teach you five cutting-edge strategies for keeping your best people.

The Simplest Steps Drive the Greatest Success

Organizations don't have trouble retaining employees because they're not creative enough or their visions aren't grand enough. In *Good to Great* Jim Collins taught us that it's not the flashy, swing-for-the-fences companies that succeed. On the contrary, it's the nose-to-the-grindstone and mistake-free companies that win.

Let's briefly digress into healthcare to see the power of that insight.

Nosocomial infections are infections acquired by patients while they're in the hospital, unrelated to the condition for which the patients were hospitalized. The Centers for Disease Control (CDC) estimates that from 5% to 15% of all hospital patients acquire some type of nosocomial infection every year (roughly 2 million patients). And nosocomial infections kill approximately 20,000 of those patients every year.

That's scary stuff, but here's the real shocker: The quickest and most effective way to reduce those 20,000 deaths, and the 2,000,000 infections, is more frequent handwashing on the part of hospital staff. The CDC says "Handwashing is the single most important means of preventing the spread of infection." A few years ago, *The New England Journal of Medicine* reported on a handwashing study in an intensive-care unit. Despite special education and monitored observation, handwashing rates were as low as 30% and never went above 48%!

It is estimated that there are over 80 million cases of food poisoning in the United States each year, resulting in as many as 10,000 deaths. Study after study indicates that inadequate handwashing is responsible for as much as 40% of those foodborne illnesses.

What's the point of all this? First, wash your hands frequently. Second, tens of thousands of lives could be saved every year if people just washed their hands. It wouldn't require a major fund drive or a worldwide benefit concert or a government initiative. It just requires every person taking 5 minutes a day to wash their hands.

Improving your retention efforts requires an equivalent effort. In this book we're not going to recommend a worldwide benefit concert or some other grandiose gesture. You don't have to rewrite your compensation plans or spend six-figures on outside consultants. We're going to point out 5 simple mistakes that most leaders and organizations make, and we're going to give you simple and straightforward techniques for correcting them.

It boggles the mind that a lack of handwashing kills so many people every year. And you might be just as surprised when you see the retention mistakes that leaders and organizations make. But like handwashing, the solutions we're going to show you are easy to understand and implement. And also like handwashing, if you correct a few mistakes and implement a few scripts and techniques, you will achieve extraordinary results.

We've taught these techniques in 1 or 2-day seminars to thousands of organizations around the world. (And tens of thousands of leaders have seen them via our Webinars and CDs). We've seen individual leaders and entire organizations transform their retention efforts and achieve remarkable success in less than 30 days. This book will teach you those lessons.

The techniques aren't complicated. If you avoid the Deadly Sins of Employee Retention, you will achieve benchmark results. If you get your colleagues onboard, your whole organization will be transformed.

We wish you great success. And remember to wash your hands.

DEADLY SIN #1:
TREATING EVERYONE EQUALLY

Imagine you're the Director of the Emergency Room at a large downtown hospital. It's a Saturday night and the evening shift is just coming on. You're expecting tonight to be busy because it's a full moon, and it's always crazy on a full moon. All of a sudden the receptionist runs into your office and tells you that Pat, one of your nurses, just called in and quit. But you employ two nurses named Pat, both of whom are scheduled to work tonight. One of them is a brilliant nurse, respected by staff, doctors and patients. The other Pat is mediocre at best, and a real thorn-in-your-side most of the time. Which of these nurses' departures will hurt you (and which one might actually help you)?

Imagine you run a 5-star restaurant. It's a Friday afternoon, you're several hours from opening for dinner, and tonight the restaurant is fully booked. While you're sitting in your office, your secretary rushes in and tells you that there's a nasty message on the voicemail from Bob, quitting his job and vowing never to set foot in your restaurant again. The problem is that you employ two guys named Bob, both of whom are scheduled to work tonight. One Bob is your head chef and the other is a busboy. Which of these Bob's departures could irreparably damage your restaurant?

The Declaration of Independence tells us that everyone is created equal. And from a moral and political perspective, we couldn't agree more. But from an organizational perspective, just because we were all created equal doesn't mean we end up that way. In the eyes of customers, some individuals are more important than others and some job categories are more important than others. And some individuals and job categories can more directly and significantly impact your organization's success (or failure).

Stop Calculating Turnover

Have you ever seen a soap opera with twins? They're always played by the same actor, so they look exactly alike on the surface. But when you peel back that perfectly coifed veneer, one twin is always good, and the other is always evil (and usually trying to kill the good twin). If a soap opera can have a moral, twins could represent the lesson "appearances can be deceiving."

Why the digression into soap operas? Because turnover statistics are the soap opera twins of the business world.

Imagine you're about to have major surgery and you have a choice of hospitals: AnyTown Hospital or MyTown Medical Center. Both have new facilities, TV ads that tug at your heartstrings and exactly the same annual turnover rates—16 percent. They're so outwardly indistinguishable that if this were all the information you had available, you'd have to flip a coin to choose between them.

But let's pretend that you do a little investigating, and you find that while these hospitals look the same on the outside, they're very different inside. While they have the same overall turnover, AnyTown Hospital's turnover is heaviest in roles like housekeepers, kitchen staff, and financial office personnel (while very few nurses and pharmacists leave). But at MyTown Medical Center, turnover is heaviest in nursing and pharmacist roles (while housekeepers and kitchen staff rarely leave).

Here's one more bit of information (and what follows is frighteningly true, not hypothetical). The Institute of Medicine (a group of the smartest researchers studying the healthcare industry) estimates that up to 98,000 people die in American hospitals every year from preventable medical errors. Yes, we said preventable medical errors. These deaths are the result of both system failures and human errors, and can include infections caused by insufficient handwashing, misinterpreted handwritten prescriptions, inconsistent application of known clinical best practices, and more. The point is that nurses and pharmacists are better able to prevent these errors than housekeepers and kitchen staff.

Have you discovered the evil twin? Both hospitals look the same (16% turnover), but one of these hospitals is much more likely to kill you (MyTown Medical Center). Turnover numbers, as they're typically calculated, don't tell you much.

Even if we knew which job roles were suffering the greatest turnover, we'd still be missing information about whether we were losing high performers or low performers.

Imagine you're a stock analyst for a Wall Street research firm and your job is to determine whether certain companies are doing well or about to fail. You've been researching a large software company (we'll call them Mircospot). You just got a tip that 400 programmers have abruptly left the company. Before you can write your analysis about how the loss of these 400 programmers will impact Mircospot, you should probably ask a few questions. Any ideas? Here's a question we'd like to ask: *Were these 400 programmers high performers or low performers?*

As the saying goes: There are lies, damn lies, and statistics. Before you get too fixated on a number, make sure it's telling you what you think it's telling you.

Some People Are More Important Than Others

When Michael Jordan played for the Chicago Bulls, an assistant coach caught Michael after a practice and chastised him for being too selfish. "Michael," he said "there's no I in TEAM." Michael stopped, looked at the coach quizzically and replied "No, but there is in WIN."

Some **individuals** are more important than others, and some **job categories** are more important than others. Let's start with individuals. Do you have an employee you'd like to clone? A high performer who's always early, anticipates your every request, is dependable, unflappable, handles pressure, stays late, and delivers exceptional service to your customers? Someone who closes deals, saves lives, fixes and prevents problems, and provides informal leadership to other employees?

Do you also know their evil twin? A low performer who's chronically late, complains constantly, resists change, questions every directive, and isn't very good at their job? Someone who chases away customers, traumatizes patients, destroys productivity and morale, and makes leaders' lives more difficult?

When you go to your favorite restaurant, are you hoping for the chef who lives to create culinary masterpieces or the chef who frequently scratches himself and believes in the 5-second rule? When you go to the bank, are you hoping for the teller who's efficient and cheerful or the teller who's as fast and friendly as a three-legged tortoise with a toothache?

High performers matter more than low performers. And every study, ours included, indicates that the more an organization focuses on retaining high performers and eliminating low performers, the more successful that organization will be.

Retention isn't just about individuals, however. It's also about knowing which job categories are most critical to your survival. Customers may consider some job categories more important than others. Some labor markets are tighter than others. Some job categories are simply harder and more expensive to replace. Some jobs require years of education and on-the-job training before an individual can be considered competent. And for some jobs there is no formal education, just years of company-specific training and on-the-job apprenticeship.

Nurses, pharmacists, respiratory therapists and radiologic technicians are in short supply in almost every region. Skilled trades like plumbers, electricians, and welders can be tough to find. Current global shortages for engineers and programmers are forecasted to slow the growth of entire economies, let alone individual companies.

Then there are jobs like Crystal Cutter. These are the folks who create the intricate designs on the fancy crystal vases and champagne flutes displayed so beautifully (if idly) in your china cabinet. It can take 7-10 years to become a master cutter.

Or take the job of Enterprise Software Architect. One of our technology clients develops proprietary software applications for organizing responses to large-scale disasters (yes, it's a rapid growth business). Even their most seasoned hires can require 6 months of on-the-job tutoring before they understand the ins-and-outs of their applications.

Where To Put Your Retention Efforts

Assuming you've got limited time and money with which to retain your most important people, where do you expend your resources? High performers are obviously more important to keep than low performers. And hard-to-replace jobs are more important than easy-to-replace jobs. But how do you reconcile these two issues?

Retention Priority Map

	Low	Medium	High
High Performer	Medium-Low Priority	Medium Priority	Top Priority
Middle Performer	Low Priority	Medium Priority	Top Priority
Low Performer	Low Priority	Low Priority	Low Priority

Costly, difficult, disruptive to replace

The Retention Priority Map tells us where we should be putting our time, for the sake of the organization's success and our customers' loyalty. On the horizontal axis is the difficulty of replacing this role. Nurses, welders, and specialized software engineers might be costly, disruptive and difficult to replace (and thus fall in the High category).

On the vertical axis is the level of performance for a particular individual. If we want to clone this person, they're a high performer. And if we're wondering what sins we committed in a past life to deserve this person, they're a low performer. (If they're somewhere in between, you've probably got a middle performer).

One twist you'll notice is that a high performer in an easier-to-replace role can be a lesser priority than a middle performer in a tough-to-replace role. In a market where pharmacists are impossible to find, your average pharmacist is going to emerge as a higher retention priority than your superstar financial analyst (assuming financial analysts are easier to find).

The market has a lot to say about where we put our retention efforts. If the market says "nurses are in very short supply," and you know that it's going to be costly, time consuming and highly disruptive to your patients if you lose a nurse, then you absolutely have to retain your nurses, even if they're just middle performers. But remember, no matter how scarce a role may be, if the individual in that role is a low performer, they're never a retention priority.

The key to retention is balancing the need for high performers in every role and the demands of often volatile labor markets. Follow the Retention Priority Map and you'll know where to focus your retention efforts.

Putting It Together

Let's look at a well-known package delivery company we'll call BrownEx (think big trucks rushing around town delivering packages with a guaranteed delivery time). One of their top priority jobs is the Delivery Driver. Drivers are the frontlines of customer service and maintain the closest customer relationships. Drivers also drive BrownEx's profitability (and thus their profits). While the company employs advanced route-mapping software to guide drivers from one delivery to another, anyone who's ever used Mapquest knows that there's the "by the book" route and then there's the best (and fastest) route. The fastest routes are idiosyncratic and usually involve alleys, side streets, avoiding certain intersections, etc. Not only are the routes idiosyncratic, but the customers are as well. Some customers are always late, some are always early, some always have heavy packages, some just send overnight envelopes, etc.

The bottom line is that it can take months for a Driver to learn the idiosyncrasies of the routes and the customers. So losing a Driver is incredibly disruptive to the organization.

But losing Drivers is just what was happening. BrownEx had high turnover in the Driver job and worse, was losing high and middle performers. So they started analyzing the situation (using techniques you'll learn in the next few chapters) and discovered that a major source of Driver flight was loading the trucks. It turns out that not only did Drivers have to deliver the packages, they also had to load the trucks before their routes started. Imagine being a driver in Dallas in the summer, loading trucks in 100 degree heat in a thick, dark uniform and then sticking to a vinyl seat for an hour as you enter the parking lot known as rush hour.

The obvious solution was simply to eliminate the loading activities from the driver's job and give them to somebody else. But would anyone take the loading activities? It's hot, sweaty, back-breaking work, and whoever does that work is not going to stay with the company for very long.

Turns out none of that matters. The loading work is inexpensive, easy to learn (30 minutes vs. several months), and doesn't require any special degrees or licenses. And you can employ students, part-timers, or basically anyone with a pulse who can lift 50 pounds. In short, if this role has high turnover, it doesn't matter.

BrownEx created this new Loader role, and as soon as they did, driver turnover went down. In fact, they cut driver turnover by 50% in under 6 months. Sure, the turnover for loaders is about 200%, but they're so easy to replace and train, it doesn't matter. BrownEx kept their most valuable people (customers love them and the company needs them), and that's what makes them successful.

Some individuals and some job categories are more important than others. When you can figure out who's who, and retain the people that keep you in business, you've just left your competition in the dust. And that's what counts.

Quiz: Are You Committing Deadly Sin #1?

Directions: Read each of the following statements. If a statement sounds like something you do or would do, or if you agree with it, circle True. If a statement does not sound like something you do or would do, or if you do not agree with it, circle False.

1.	In terms of retention efforts, I treat my high and low performers equally.	*True False*
2.	I believe that the greatest retention efforts should always be focused on the high performers.	*True False*
3.	I think turnover rates say a lot about a company.	*True False*
4.	I'm unsure which job roles in my company are harder to fill.	*True False*
5.	All employees are equally important in the eyes of customers.	*True False*

Scoring: Give yourself 1 point for each True response and 0 points for each False response.

Interpreting Your Score
0 = You are not committing Deadly Sin #1
1 – 2 = You are in danger of committing Deadly Sin #1
3 – 5 = You are committing Deadly Sin #1

DEADLY SIN #2:
ONE SIZE FITS ALL

Paul, Christine, Bill and Sue are all financial analysts at Stay-Healthy Inc., a large Midwestern insurance company. They're all around 40 years old, they all have kids, they all drink coffee, they're all married, they've all tried Atkins and South Beach diets, and they all went to college and graduate school. In short, these folks are pretty demographically similar. But, that doesn't mean they're motivated by the same things.

Paul is driven by money. Not by ostentatious displays of wealth, but by having financial security (i.e. money in the bank). He doesn't care about the particulars of his job; he'd do whatever job pays him the most money. When the new pay-for-performance plan went into effect, his job performance shot right up. The bigger the bonus, the harder he works. Of course, without that plan, he'd likely be out the door tomorrow.

Christine is easily bored. She's an adrenaline junkie and needs to do interesting and cutting-edge work. If there's a new or experimental project, she's all over it. Also, she doesn't much care for stupid people, and thus often works by herself. Give her a risky project with lots of autonomy, and she's ecstatic. Put her with a large group of mediocre minds doing boring work, and she's ready to take a header off her cubicle wall.

Bill is driven by a need to feel good about himself and the work he does. Ever since the birth of his daughter he's been gripped by a sense of existential inadequacy. He's concerned with making the world a better place and showing his little princess that he makes a difference. Last month he worked on a project that developed creative ways to offer health insurance to very poor families, and he was more driven and productive than he's ever been.

Sue needs control. She's emotionally attached to her work area and her work product. And she is not a fan of people messing with "her area." She's territorial, but very competent. When she's in control, she's highly motivated. If she lost that control, she'd lose her desire to work for Stay-Healthy Inc.

Imagine that you manage Paul, Christine, Bill and Sue. How do you retain them? Is an organization-wide, or even a department-wide, strategy going to work? How about a new pay-for-performance plan, or flexible work schedules, or an organization-wide raise? Is there any one cure-all approach that will work?

The Fallacy of the "Average Person"

Both of the authors were raised in Buffalo, NY. While we eventually moved further south to escape the intense winters, we remain die-hard fans of the Buffalo Bills. So we're going to use a sports example to make a point. The average NFL player weighs 245 pounds and is 6'1½" tall. *(We knew NFL players were pretty big guys, so nothing shocking here.)* But what's fascinating is that there is not one single player on the Buffalo Bills who either weighs 245 pounds or is 6'1½" tall. And of course, there are no players who match <u>both</u> averages (i.e. weighs 245 pounds <u>and</u> is 6'1½" tall).

One day we assigned one of our researchers to scour the rosters of every NFL team looking for the average player (weighs 245 pounds <u>and</u> is 6'1½" tall). It was pretty tedious work, so we let him stop after 10 teams, but he was unable to find even one player that matched the NFL average.

What's the point of this exercise? Averages lie. Averages are misleading. Nobody is "average" and if you go looking for the "average" person, you will probably never find them. (Have you ever seen a family with 2.5 kids?)

This same "Fallacy of the Average Person" holds true when we're talking about employee retention. Some people quit their organization because they don't like their hours. Some desire more flexibility. Some want better benefits, while others want more cash in their pockets. Some can't stand their boss, others dislike their coworkers. Some want career advancement, others want to do their current job without being pushed to climb any higher. Like the StayHealthy, Inc. folks in our opening example, everyone is driven by something a little different.

In the 1997 book *The War for Talent*, consultants from McKinsey & Company asked thousands of managers and executives "What are the critical factors in your decision to join and stay at an organization?" As you might expect, the answers were all over the place. Some folks said it's interesting and challenging work; others said it's work I feel passionate about; some said it's career advancement opportunities; others said it's the company's long-term commitment to me. Other popular answers included: whether the company is well managed; good relations with my boss; I like the culture and values; the physical location is appealing; it's a reasonable work pace; high performers get paid more; the annual cash compensation is high. McKinsey's total list comprised 40 issues.

If you look at exit interview studies you find similar results. In organization-wide studies people usually say they quit for reasons that include lack of recognition or rewards; lack of advancement opportunities; lack of feedback from management; not being made to feel like a valued employee; lack of training and education; uncompetitive compensation; and lack of responsibility.

If you can distill these responses into one universal reason people stay or quit an organization you deserve a medal. We've tried and it just doesn't work.

We hope we've made the point that people are unique and tend to be motivated by different things. But most organizations still haven't gotten the message. Every day we see companies implement organization-wide strategies that utilize a limited number of techniques to retain the entire work force (desperately hoping to find that "average" employee).

For example, in the past few months we've seen numerous hospitals institute retention programs centered on creating flexible work-shifts for nurses. It's not that flexible shifts are an inherently bad idea, it's just that not everyone actually cares about it or finds it motivating. So these organizations spend hundreds of thousands of dollars (and incalculable hours) to rewrite entire systems and policies to accommodate the retention needs of a few employees.

The problem goes beyond the fact that this is an amazingly inefficient way to retain people. While these organizations institute the new systems, they're ignoring the needs of everyone else. If 20% of the workforce is going to be retained because the organization instituted this new system (and that's being very generous), what happens to the other 80% that got missed? What about their retention needs? Are we willing to let these people walk out the door?

McKinsey found 40 factors that drove people's willingness to stay. And we're going to institute a system that only tackles one of those factors? If a patient arrived in the Emergency Room suffering from 40 stab wounds, are we only going to treat one of those wounds and hope that the other 39 will take care of themselves?

As if this weren't enough, there's one more complicating factor we have to address. There are a decent number of cases where people just don't know why they stay or leave. The things that drive them in or out of an organization are operating on a subconscious level.

Let's take a classic case in which we have a highly-gifted programmer who gets promoted to manager. It turns out that this programmer-turned-manager is a terrible manager. (As we all know, the best programmer, the best nurse, the best engineer, or the best welder does not always make the best manager). This guy is terrible at being a manager, and he's deeply unhappy. But he doesn't realize that it's the new job that's making him unhappy. So he now begins to think it's the company that's making him unhappy, and he quits. He joins another company, but this time he joins it as a manager, not as a programmer. The cycle of unhappiness starts all over again, and he quits this new job as well. And on and on the cycle goes.

This whole section is leading up to our argument for radically changing how we retain our employees. We had to be thorough here because, notwithstanding all this evidence, most managers refuse to accept that every individual is unique. Many managers have difficulty grasping the idea that every individual stays and quits for very different reasons. 89% of managers believe that money is the biggest reason why employees quit. We've asked thousands of managers "Why did your employees quit?" and overwhelmingly they say "My employees quit because somebody else offered them more money." Of course, as you can guess from the previous pages, most employees don't quit because of the money. Some do, but 91% of employees say money had nothing to do with their decision to leave.

One Size Fits One

We hope we've made it clear that there is no universal, magical, silver-bullet, cure-all retention tactic that works for every employee. If there was, we wouldn't need this book. Instead we'd write a book called *The Magic Answer to Retention: Do This and Everybody Stays*. And it'd be about 10 pages long (and sell for a million dollars).

The only retention approach that can succeed is to engage each employee 1:1. If we want to figure out why people stay and/or leave, we're going to have to ask them. The greatest organizations, the ones who do the best job of retaining their top people, spend the most time engaging 1:1 with their employees.

When we talk about engaging employees 1:1, what we're really talking about is a conversation between the manager and an individual employee to diagnose what drives them (what keeps them here and what could make them quit). It can be in an office, over coffee, over lunch, or anywhere two people can have a reasonably private conversation for at least 20 minutes. And just to be clear, we're also talking about a conversation that takes place at least once every quarter (although once a month is even better).

Of course, if we're talking about folks that we'd love to see quit the organization, then we're not going to worry too much about having these quarterly conversations. But for the folks we want to keep, for our top and medium priorities (as identified in the previous chapter), we need quarterly conversations at a minimum. The benchmark organizations, and the benchmark leaders, conduct these conversations at least once a month. But if you start with every quarter, you'll be far ahead of your competitors.

Finally, these are mandatory conversations. If retaining your most important employees is an organizational priority, these conversations must be a managerial priority. Later in the chapter we'll show you how to institute these conversations as a mandatory procedure, but for now it's sufficient to say that every leader must commit to these conversations, from the CEO on down.

Shoves and Tugs

These conversations can be pretty simple. We're really only interested in asking about two issues – Shoves and Tugs. Shoves are the issues that make people leave. Tugs are the issues that make people stay.

Why do we need to ask about both issues? Aren't they the same thing? The answer is No. People quit for a certain set of reasons, and they stay for a different set of reasons. Only asking *why people leave* is insufficient, and only asking *why people stay* is insufficient. We need to know <u>both</u> what could frustrate employees and shove them out the door <u>and</u> what really drives them and tugs at them to stay with the organization.

Shoves tend to be focused on basic issues like working conditions, schedules, compensation, acceptable relationship with the boss, etc. Tugs often encompass higher-order issues like enjoying the work, career advancement, working with interesting people, organizational culture, etc.

This tends to be a radical concept for most leaders, so let's walk through an example. Pat is a nurse at a major teaching hospital. She's worked there for 8 years, and thinks it's a great place to work. She loves doing research, and this organization has hundreds of ongoing studies on which she can participate, and even publish. Her major Tug is doing intellectually challenging work with really smart people. But two weeks ago, the hospital instituted flexible work schedules and they changed all the shifts. This is causing Pat serious difficulty because she had timed her kids' schedules around her old shift start/end times, and now this disrupts everything. For Pat, this scheduling change is a Shove.

If we had only asked Pat what excited her about her job, what really made her love this hospital, we'd have gotten an answer about doing intellectually stimulating work. And if we had only asked Pat what could make her life sufficiently miserable to cause her resignation, we'd have gotten an answer about her schedule and her outside-of-work obligations. It's only when we ask about both issues that we get the complete picture.

When you're working with low performers, when you're working terrible hours, or you've got a terrible working environment, you could be so frustrated that you feel like you're being Shoved out the door. You could feel so frustrated that you no longer notice all of the other good things about your job that Tug at you to stay – the autonomy, the ability to have control over an entire process, the ability to work on innovative projects and teams. If you're like the organizations in our studies, as much as 35% of your workforce could feel this way. And these people are huge retention risks.

On the other hand, you could have a working environment free from Shoves, but also lacking any significant Tugs. You're not being Shoved out the door by frustration, but neither are you being Tugged to remain at the company. If you're like the organizations in our studies, as much as 50%

of your workforce could feel this way. The good news is that these people probably aren't spending their days on Monster.com actively applying for jobs. The bad news is that if the economy changes, or one of your competitors makes a play for them, or they just happen across another opportunity, they will leave.

To get someone really truly committed to your organization, you must eliminate any Shoves and fulfill at least some of their Tugs. In essence, you've got to meet their basic needs and afford some opportunity to address their higher-order needs.

What Do You Actually Ask?

When you sit down with each employee to talk about their Shoves and Tugs, it's a good idea to have some questions already in mind. So the following are some of the most effective questions. Let's start with the Shoves...

Shoves Questions

Indirect Questions
- Do you know any employees who have left?
- Do you know why they left?
- What are the 2-3 things you think other employees like least about this organization?
- Can you imagine reasons why employees would leave this company?

Direct Questions
- In the past 90 days, can you tell me about a time you felt really unmotivated or demotivated?
- When was the last time you felt really demotivated?
- What are the 2-3 things you like least about this organization?
- If somebody asked you about the single worst part of working here, what would it be?
- Has there been a point in the past 90 days when you've felt like leaving? What caused it?

Blunt Questions
- Have you thought about quitting?
- Are you thinking about quitting?

Mandatory Question
- If you felt demotivated again, would you feel comfortable sharing that with me?

You don't need to ask all of these questions to get the information you need, so start by picking the style of question that feels most comfortable: Indirect, Direct or Blunt. Our experience is that about 15% of managers have a sufficiently strong bond with their employees to ask the Blunt Questions. We've probably all had those relationships with some key employees that transcended boss-subordinate relationships and became a real friendship. However, if you don't know with certainty that you could sit down with them and ask the Blunt Questions, then we recommend using the Direct or Indirect Questions.

The Direct Questions were designed to prompt behavioral responses. We want people to think about specific incidents and situations, because most people do a lousy job of answering hypotheticals. When employees get specific, you get much more insight. The Indirect Questions were designed to be projective. Because some people feel intimidated answering Direct questions, the Indirect Questions give them the option of talking about someone else. Of course, anyone with teenage kids (or anyone who's ever been a teenager) knows that talking about "my friend" is tantamount to talking about yourself.

Regardless of the questions you use, just be sure to always ask the mandatory question: *If you felt demotivated again, would you feel comfortable sharing that with me?* This question not only tests your relationship with each employee, it also tells them that you want a closer relationship. And this will ensure that if they ever feel like quitting, you'll hear about it in enough time to stop them from quitting.

When we teach this topic in our live seminars, there's one question that someone in the audience always asks: *By asking these questions, aren't I making my employees think about quitting? Aren't I putting ideas in their head?*

It's a very natural question, and here's our answer. Just because you have an EKG at a checkup doesn't mean you're more likely to have a heart attack. Just because you get screened for breast or prostate cancer doesn't mean you're more likely to get those cancers. If you're at risk of a heart attack, getting a good cardiac workup will uncover all those hidden risks. It may feel scary to learn that your risk is so high (and that's why so many people don't get the necessary tests), but the tests don't cause the illness. So the real question is whether you'd rather bury your head in the sand and just hope your employees don't quit, or raise the issues, discover the risks, and start working to retain them. And remember, your employees quit someone else to join your organization, so it's not like they don't understand the concept.

Now let's look at the Tugs Questions...

Tugs Questions

Indirect Questions
- What are the 2-3 things you think other employees like best about this organization?

Direct Questions
- In the past 90 days, can you tell me about a time you felt really motivated or excited?
- When was the last time you felt really motivated?
- What got you excited?
- What are the 2-3 things you like best about this organization?
- Why do you think employees stay at this company?
- Can you tell me about why you joined the organization?
- If you had to tell somebody about the single best part of working here, what would it be?
- Is there anything that would improve your working experience?

Blunt Question
- How do you feel about your opportunities for success here?

Mandatory Question
- Is there anything that would improve your working experience that you think is out of my control?

The Tugs Questions are designed to find out what's likely to make your employees stay. What gets them really excited about this company? As with the Shoves Questions, pick the style that feels most comfortable.

And of course, ask the Mandatory Question: *Is there anything that would improve your working experience that you think is out of my control?* This is an absolutely critical question that most untrained managers would never think to ask. The reason we ask this is that employees often stay silent on issues they believe their manager doesn't have the authority to address. And these issues are often some of the most important issues to them. It's unfortunate that we actually have to ask this question, but a great many employees have a pretty dim view as to what their manager can and cannot control.

Bear in mind that we're not asking these questions simply for the sake of asking questions; we actually want to know the answers. (In the next section we'll address what to do with the answers). And what you'll typically find is that the issues surfaced by these questions are as different as people's hair colors or their choice of ties. Each person is a little bit different, so we want to know what drives them, what keeps them, and what's going to make them leave, so that we can take the necessary steps to retain them.

Taking Action

The first to-do we suggest is for every manager create a summary of their conversations. For each employee, we want to know their potential shoves, their potential tugs, and their overall risk for departure – high, medium and low. We want to identify the issues that need fixing, and if it looks like it will have a positive Return on Investment (ROI), then we're going to do whatever it takes to keep them.

You're probably wondering: *How do I know if something will have a positive ROI?* Essentially we're going to ask "Is the cost of losing this person greater than the cost of keeping this person?" The cost of losing somebody can include their relationships, experience, customer bonds, impact on the customers, time and effort to replace them, money to replace them, etc. And the costs of keeping somebody can include everything involved in solving their particular Shove; money, time, resentment from other employees, etc. Typically, the cost of losing someone is much more expensive than the cost of keeping them. So we're generally going to try and fix their Shoves. Every so often it will cost too much to try and fix their Shoves, and in those rare instances, you'll immediately start planning to replace them.

If there's one hallmark of the managers with the best retention rates, the folks who've never lost a high performer, it's their pragmatism. They don't stand on ceremony. When they find a Shove, they fix it. If the Shove is that their leadership style is too micromanaging, they take a leadership course and they stop micromanaging. If the Shove for one of your high performers is that they're spending too much time working with low performers, they change work assignments or workgroups. In the BrownEx example from the previous chapter, leaders redesigned entire job roles to eliminate a Shove.

By the way, notwithstanding that you're going to hear different answers from every employee, you may start to identify some themes. If there are Shoves endemic to you as a leader, or your department or even your organization, you may hear those. And when you do, they need to be tackled just as swiftly as if it were a solitary issue.

For the Low and Medium departure risks, you've got 30 days to start fixing their Shoves. But if the person is at High risk of departure, you've only got 3 days. If someone is about to quit, or their frustration is off-the-chart, you don't have much time.

High risk employees are pretty easy to identify. They might just tell you that they're actively considering leaving (or they've actively considered leaving in the past 90 days). Other warning signs include wistful talk about others who have left, becoming withdrawn and not engaging in the conversation, acting like they've got something to hide, and more negative comments than you would typically expect from this person.

Once you've eliminated the critical Shoves, take the same approach with the Tugs. Find issues you can tackle that have a positive ROI, and just get going.

The reason why this approach is so effective is that people will tell you exactly why they'll stay and exactly why they'll leave. You don't have to guess, you don't have to spend millions of dollars doing surveys to figure it out. All you have to do is ask a few questions, listen to the answers and take action wherever you can.

Putting It Together

The final question is, "How did StayHealthy Inc. keep Paul, Christine, Bill and Sue?" Their manager mapped out all of their, shoves, tugs, and risk level for leaving, and came up with individual action plans for each of them. They were each interviewed utilizing the Shoves & Tugs Questions and their needs were identified.

Employee	Shoves	Tugs	Risk of Leaving	To Do:
Paul	No administrative support	Financial Security/ Money	Low	Get Paul access to support staff for a couple hours per week
Christine	Group work Repetitive tasks	Creative work Autonomy	Medium	Give Christine choices over which projects she takes on. Limit time with teams. Give solo projects when possible.
Bill	Working late Missing family events	Social Values	Medium	Allow flexible schedule for family events. Set due dates but allow for some working from home. Assign to more "social value" projects.
Sue	Lack of personal space Few chances to lead	Being in charge Leadership	High	Discuss track for managerial position. Trials as team leader

After interviewing Paul, it appeared that he was pretty content at the moment. He was very motivated by the current pay-for-performance plan, and was feeling really positive about his success. His only Shove was a suggestion that he could produce even more if he had some help with his paperwork. In the end, his manager decided that some of the more menial paperwork tasks could be delegated to an intern.

Christine and Bill were more moderate risks. Christine was getting bored with some of the team tasks she was assigned to, and Bill was feeling taxed by the late hours he was putting in that cut into his family time. While team tasks couldn't be eliminated, Christine could be given more choice about which team tasks she preferred to take on. Additionally, she was given the chance to "prove herself" on an new cross-departmental project. Bill was given the option to work from home one day per week, and flexible scheduling was discussed. He was also offered more choice about which projects he preferred.

Sue, on the other hand, was at high risk of leaving. It was discerned that she really wants to move up in the organization, and she sees herself as a leader. She likes to be "in charge" and has worked extremely well as a leader. But she's had few opportunities to lead. She also disliked her cubicle arrangement with its lack of privacy. Since Sue has good potential as a leader, it was discussed with her that she could be put up for promotion if she demonstrates excellent productivity and leadership skills over the next six months. A promotion would mean a managerial position and a private office. Her manager spelled-out very clearly what Sue would need to do, and how she would need to act.

In sum, maximizing the Tugs and minimizing the Shoves keeps employees tied to their organization. Each person has their own unique Shoves and Tugs, and these Shoves and Tugs are not static. What StayHealthy, Inc. has shown us is that "One Size Fits One" and that, like our waistlines over the years, sizes are always changing.

Quiz: Are You Committing Deadly Sin #2?

Directions: Read each of the following statements. If a statement sounds like something you do or would do, or if you agree with it, circle True. If a statement does not sound like something you do or would do, or if you do not agree with it, circle False.

1. My organization relies on broad organization-wide initiatives to try to retain employees.	*True False*
2. I often don't know why my employees quit.	*True False*
3. I can guess why each employee quit.	*True False*
4. Knowing why employees would leave is equivalent to knowing why they would stay.	*True False*
5. Most employees can be motivated by the same things.	*True False*

Scoring: Give yourself 1 point for each True response and 0 points for each False response.

Interpreting Your Score
0 = You are not committing Deadly Sin #2
1 – 2 = You are in danger of committing Deadly Sin #2
3 – 5 = You are committing Deadly Sin #2

DEADLY SIN #3:
NEGLECTING THE FIRST 90 DAYS

Imagine you're the Vice President of Sales at a national cellular phone company. You just hired Roger, who was a high performing salesman at a local electronics store. He came from a small, personal environment, where he was the top dog. Now he needs to navigate the bureaucracy of your large firm and start out at the bottom. As you walk him into your office, and remember the nightmare that was your first month on the job here, you wonder if Roger is going to stay or bolt. What can you do to make the transition easier for Roger? How do you keep him from running?

The reality is that turnover rates in the first 90 days are higher than for any other period of employment. Leadership IQ studies have found a wide range of early turnover, from as low as 2% to as high as 50% in some companies. Our studies also found that companies whose leaders focus on building bonds with their employees in the first 90 days retain more employees during that initial period, and tend to retain them longer over all. What we have learned from those companies is to *put out the welcome mat* and *initiate them into the family.*

Put Out The Welcome Mat

Before your new hire even steps through the door, you want them to feel welcomed, wanted, and prepared for the start of their career at your organization. Before day one comes, send a card. Given our propensity for card-driven holidays, you probably won't be shocked to learn that American Greetings makes a "Welcome" card for new employees. Get or make a card, get all your employees to sign it, and send it to your new employee's home. This is done so rarely that this one simple gesture ensures that they'll be feeling excited about joining your team. You'll also eliminate any regrets they may have had about quitting their previous job. And just as importantly, you'll win-over their spouse or partner (a critical, and usually ignored, factor in every employee's decision-making about whether to join or leave an organization).

When you're excited and/or anxious about a new situation, do you conduct some extra research? If you're about to take your first African safari, wouldn't you buy some travel books and do some reading? Or spend a few hours Googling African safaris? Of course you would. And that's just how your new employees feel (in fact, starting a new job is a lot like a safari). So this is a great time to give them some of the key reading materials – the handbook, any marketing materials, the policies and procedures. Because they're excited, and a little anxious, they're much more likely to read now than they at any other point in employment. And this will make them feel a little better.

Another great idea is to assemble a roster of your current team. Don't make it too serious or intimidating, but provide a basic "who's who." The best ones we've seen include everyone's name, title, years of service, one sentence about their job functions, and then something off-the-wall like their favorite tree or vacation or food. The trick is to give the new employee something really memorable to read, and nothing accomplishes that like humor. It also disarms them and makes your staff seem approachable. Finally, it's a good idea to stay away from things that might make the lawyers unhappy, like religion, race, sex, medical history, etc.

Also, tell your employees that a new employee is joining the team. It's truly remarkable how many managers forget to tell their current employees that a new employee is arriving. So prep them. Schedule meetings with all of your team members, and make sure that every current employee attends. In the meeting you need to prep current staff and assuage whatever fears and anxieties they may have. You want to make sure that the team is going to be friendly and helpful, not unwelcoming and antagonistic.

First impressions count for a lot, and teams have been known to sabotage new hires out of loyalty to former colleagues or competitiveness or cliquishness. The best way to get teams to be friendly is to have each person pick one thing they can do to welcome the new employee. Then pick someone (or ask for a volunteer) to be the new hire's "buddy" and acclimate them to the team and the organization.

Finally, ensure your calendar is open on their first day. There is nothing worse than starting a new job where your boss is in meetings all day and you've been relegated to filling out forms in the break room.

Initiate Them Into The Family

Day 1 Morning: When your new employee shows up, meet with them the second they walk through the door. If you're their manager, make sure they come right to you.

Many organizations make orientation the very first contact with the organization. They send the employees to a designated training room, away from the people with whom they'll be working, and start the indoctrination. We're fine with starting the orientation in the afternoon, but the morning tends to be a bad idea.

Have you ever seen nature films where the baby duck hatches and bonds to the first creature it sees, even if it's not a duck? New employees are the same way. They're excited and a little anxious, and they're going to reach out to, and bond with, the first person who reciprocates. Many organizations say "we want people bonded to the organization, not individual managers, so that's why orientation comes first." It's a lovely sentiment, but it ignores reality. You can bond people to other people, not to companies. We all know the old adage: You join a company, but quit a manager. And as we've demonstrated throughout this book, it's very true.

If you're the manager of this new employee, here's one more disturbing thought. If your employee starts bonding with other new hires from their orientation class, they may be bonded to people who are working for terrible managers. So your new employee's perspective could be distorted and attempts to bond with them jeopardized. Yes, you can undo this contamination, but why exert all that extra effort if you can avoid the problem in the first place?

When the new hire comes to you first thing in the morning, you want to accomplish a few things. First, act as a representative of the company, and ensure that they have a good image of it. Second, give them a good image of their new colleagues and the company's leadership. This is not the time to vent your frustration and dump on your boss or the CEO. Third, tell them how important and valued their job is and how excited you are to have them in this role. Fourth, in a very positive way, give them the nutshell version of the work they'll be doing. Again, this is not the time or place to be negative or tell them about all the roadblocks they're going to encounter.

Finally, introduce them to their "buddy". What's the buddy (and why do most effective organizations have some sort of a buddy system)? The buddy is someone who meets weekly with this person for the first month and then every few weeks for the first six months or so. It is somebody to help guide them through the organization. While the manager would be the easiest and most likely choice, hierarchical power dynamics mean it's better if it's somebody other than the manager. The role of the buddy is best filled by some-one who can ask questions like: *"How's it going?" "Feeling over-whelmed?" "How can I help you be even more effective?" "Do you know where the bathrooms are?"* The buddy makes sure that the new person always has some personal connection.

We interviewed one of our benchmark leaders about her very successful buddy system, and she told us that each of her employees expects to be a buddy at some point in time, if they haven't been already. She said "I have employees that still have lunch with their buddy once a week... and they've been working together for years."

The buddy system may seem silly, but it's based on psycho-logically sound ideas. Imagine that you're a new kid in a new high school, and you're looking at all these strange faces in the cafeteria. Wouldn't it be nice if one kid came over and said "Hey, come over and eat with us?" Admit it, you'd be relieved. That's exactly the feeling we're talking about. In every study we conduct, the cruel politics of high school are not lost when we grow into adulthood and into the work-force. They still exist. Introduce the new person to as many people as you possibly can, and have those people be as wel-coming and excited as possible. Remember that people of-ten leave their old workplaces with a bang (a party and gifts), so you want them to enter their new workplace with equal fanfare.

The buddy can also orient them to all the basic procedures that we sometimes forget about. Things like how/when paychecks arrive, how to use the phones, bathroom locations, and the best local restaurants, etc.

Day 1 Afternoon: As we mentioned earlier, this is a fine time to conduct a formal orientation. If your orientation takes a full day or more, you can continue it the next day. Just make sure you catch-up with them before they leave the first day. You only need a few minutes, but you want to check-in and see how they're doing. And you must ask the following question (it's a variation on the mandatory Shoves question): *I know starting a new job can feel overwhelming, but if you ever feel overwhelmed or frustrated or even like quitting, will you feel comfortable sharing that with me?*

Asking this question builds a psychological bond and a sense of obligation. So if your new hire ever feels like quitting, they're significantly more likely to come and talk to you.

Week 1: Sometime during their first week, we suggest having a pizza party or ice cream or lunch out or something similar. Remember, they probably had a party when they left their previous job, so it's nice to equal that enthusiasm at their new job. Also, if you make new hires fun for your current staff, they're much more likely to actually help new hires integrate and show them the ropes. Why do the more senior fraternity members haze the pledges? Because they were hazed themselves.

Another very successful technique is to have a senior leader stop by and greet the new employee (just make sure the executive knows the new employee's name). It's a thrill for every employee to meet the CEO or someone close (depending on the size of your organization). And nothing says "we really care about you and we're excited to have you here" than when a busy executive makes time to stop by and say "hi."

Finally, encourage your employees to complete their one welcome task. It's important to create a sense of family. For a few weeks the new person is going to feel like the redheaded step-child, but it's crucial to minimize this stage and get them "adopted" as quickly as possible. Otherwise, you risk losing them to their former family. So the best thing to do is check in with them every single day.

Month 1 – 3: Changing jobs is very stressful for most people. It is a time of upheaval and great change. It is also a chance for growth and development. During this fragile period, you, as the leader, have a chance to forge a relationship that will endure. You can build a bond that will last you a decade or more. This bonding primarily takes place in the first month. Once you've established your relationship and helped to build networks with peers or colleagues, then you can move into the first performance review.

The first performance review should be done right after the one month mark, not 90 days as is typical. The purpose of this first review is to give them guidance and let them know how they are doing. Then, you want to find out how they are doing, and what this experience has been like for them.

This is not a formal evaluation, but informal coaching and checking in. Let them know that your philosophy is to coach them to success. You want this person to succeed, so make sure that you're giving them the feedback they need to succeed. Waiting 90 days to do all of this is way too long, and most 90 day reviews are designed to evaluate probationary periods, not guide and coach.

In this coaching session you should focus on three things:

1) Praise and Goodies – Give your new hire positive feedback. First, they made it through the roughest part of being a new hire. Also pick out some specific job related tasks that they did well. Give them some positive guidance too.

2) Describe Their Experience – Ask the employee to talk about what the first month has been like for them: the good, the bad, and ideas for improvement. Maybe they could compare it to their experience as a new employee at their former job as well.

3) Clarify Expectations – Discuss their job role. Make sure they understand the expectations regarding their performance, who they work with, and what they are responsible for.

After you've gone through these three items, you can get them cycled into your Shoves & Tugs conversations.

Putting It Together

Is Roger going to stay or bolt? Luckily, you remembered to have the employee handbook sent to him ahead of time so that he could read up on the company. Then you sent a card signed by all the staff and a roster of the entire team so that he would get to know all of his coworkers. Last week you met with your sales staff and discussed Roger coming on board and got them really psyched up for his arrival. You know that Roger will be welcomed into the fold. You shake his hand as he comes into your office, and you tell him how excited you are to have him on board. You talk to him a little bit about his job role, and give him a brief rundown of what his first day will look like: Breakfast with you, an introduction to Carl- who will be his peer mentor, and then a tour of the sales department. Then off to lunch with the sales staff, and orientation with Ginny from HR, then back to your office for a short check in before he goes home. It sounds like a busy day, but Roger looks eager and happy. You've set everything in motion for a good welcome, and you have a solid plan for the next few months. The statistics are on your side. You feel confident that Roger will stay.

Quiz: Are You Committing Deadly Sin #3?

Directions: Read each of the following statements. If a statement sounds like something you do or would do, or if you agree with it, circle True. If a statement does not sound like something you do or would do, or if you do not agree with it, circle False.

1. On their first day, my new hires meet with someone else before they meet with me.	*True False*
2. New hires start off right away with an orientation.	*True False*
3. My team usually isn't prepared for a new member.	*True False*
4. We don't use a buddy/mentor system for new hires.	*True False*
5. After the first week, I don't spend much time or thought on the new hire unless they are not meeting expectations.	*True False*

Scoring: Give yourself 1 point for each True response and 0 points for each False response.

Interpreting Your Score
0 = You are not committing Deadly Sin #3
1 – 2 = You are in danger of committing Deadly Sin #3
3 – 5 = You are committing Deadly Sin #3

DEADLY SIN #4: LETTING THEM LEAVE

Imagine that you're the President of a mid-sized printing company. You're in the middle of placing a supply order when your Sales Director rushes through the door and tells you that Self-Pub just called and said they will no longer need your services. Self-Pub is one of your biggest clients and they've accounted for one-third of your revenue for the past five years. What do you do? Do you just let them go? Or do you immediately jump on the phone and work to get them back?

Now imagine that you own a home remodeling company. You're in the middle of a very large and labor intensive renovation. Jake, one of your best carpenters, solemnly approaches you at the end of the day on Friday to give you his two weeks notice. What do you do? What do you say?

If you believe that the adage "If you love somebody set them free" applies here, then you're putting yourself in a losing position. Most people are unwilling to accept a goodbye from a major client; they call them, make personal visits, send gifts, and log countless hours of wooing. Yet these same people often just roll over and play dead when an employee, even a stellar one, says that they want to leave. Why is that? What is so different about these two scenarios that cause people to respond so disparately?

In the following pages, you are going to see why it is so important to drop the whole "set them free" attitude and adopt a new saying: "Don't give up without a fight." In the next section we will spell out a 3-Step process that will have you fighting and winning the battle to keep your employees when they tell you that they want to quit.

Step 1: Slow Them Down

Quick and painless. That's what they want. Like pulling a bandage off a skinned knee. Employees generally hate giving their boss any bad news, especially if they like their boss. And telling your boss that you want to quit counts as giving bad news. So they want to give the news FAST. They want to be in and out of the office and have it over and done with.

Imagine you're the manager of a very high profile advertising project. Your skills are invaluable to the success of your team and this assignment. You've already worked with this client for over a year, the project will continue for another year, and you know all the ins-and-outs of their product line. You generally like your job and take pride in what you do. You get along very well with your boss, and feel like she has been a mentor to you. But, you have another job offer, with a big promotion, and they want you to start next month.

You need to tell your boss that you want to accept this new job offer. How do you feel? How do you feel with each successive day that goes by?

In 2004, Leadership IQ polled 217 employees who quit their job within the last year. When asked about their emotional state, 87% of the employees said they felt very anxious about telling their boss that they planned on leaving. And with each day that passed without telling, they got more and more nervous. Through further interviews we discovered that not only did they want to *feel relief from this growing nervousness*, they also wanted to *"get it over with" so that they wouldn't change their mind*.

Quitting can be a monumental decision, and employees can feel deeply conflicted and unsure about their decision to quit. So they don't want their decision challenged because they know that they could be talked out of it. Employees also feel anxious about telling their boss. So they're desperately hoping that they can tell their boss quickly, with no real conversation, and get out of the office as quickly as possible.

When employees enter your office to tell you that they quit, they're unsure, anxious, emotionally-fragile and easily swayed. They want to deliver their message as quickly as possible so they can feel emotional relief and so they don't get talked out of their decision.

The question for leaders becomes: "How do you keep them from feeling relief and in an emotionally-conflicted state where they might change their mind?" You don't want to make this easy for them. On the contrary, the more anxious and vulnerable they feel, the better your chance of changing their mind. So your first job is to *slow them down*.

Don't let them step in and out of your office, don't let them off the phone, don't let them escape. It is critical to keep them in this "discomfort zone" as long as possible. Slowing them down means slowing yourself down as well. The slowing down process has three stages.

Step 1: Withhold Relief

Stop, look, listen and question. Stop what you are doing. Find a quiet space to talk, either in your office or a meeting room. Tell them that you want to hear more about what they just told you, and do it immediately. Look at their body language. How comfortable or uncomfortable do they seem? The more uncomfortable they are, the greater the likelihood you can convince them to stay. Listen to their story. Ask to hear the whole saga. Stay neutral and listen with an open mind. Gather all the data, both flattering and unflattering, about your company and about you. Ask questions. Find out all the reasons they want to leave your company. Find out what the new position will offer them. Gather as much data as possible.

Quiet Down, Speak Up. Ask your employee to keep quiet about their potential decision for now. Get your employee to agree to keep it under wraps until you have fully fleshed out the details together. Why? Because if they don't tell people, then it isn't set in stone. What reason do you give to your employee? Let them know that you don't want them to limit their options at this point. At the same time, you need to speak to the people above you about the potential loss of this employee. It's important to tell your boss about it within an hour of your meeting with the employee. Bring the data you gathered in your listening session and brainstorm about what you might be able to do or offer to keep your employee.

24 Hour Waiting Period. At the end of your listening session with the employee, ask them to hold off on their final decision until you've had a chance to present them with all the options. Give a 24 hour waiting period, and set up a meeting for the next day. This will give you time to talk with your superiors and see what, if any, options you can offer to keep your employee.

End with Kudos. If you end your meeting on a positive note, it will be fresh on the employee's mind. Let your employee know that you appreciated his or her candor, and that they are truly a valued member of your team and that's why you want to take some time to figure out how you can keep them. The employee will likely see your efforts as a sign of their value, and may genuinely think twice about their reasons for leaving.

Step 2: Make Your Offer

It's important to set up a meeting for as early as possible the day after your employee made his or her announcement. The meeting should consist of the employee, you, and someone higher up and representing the organization. It's important to have a higher-up there (or a Board member if you're the CEO trying to retain an executive) to demonstrate your seriousness.

Before the meeting, you want to spend some time creating valid arguments that show how staying with your company is in the employee's best interest. Now, if you are thoroughly convinced that there is no valid argument, then you've lost them because you can't sell this convincingly. But if you are convinced there is a valid argument, then you might be able to address the concerns they expressed in the previous meeting. Maybe it involves a job transfer. Maybe it involves working for another manager, moving to a new department, or creating a new job. Whatever the issue is, you've got to figure out what you're going to do.

When you begin your meeting, start by stating all the concerns that they presented to you. You want to validate those concerns, but you also need to address the whole "grass is greener" issue about the new company by exposing them as unrealistic. Walk through what it's really going to be like over at that other company. You don't want to do it in a nasty, blaming way, but you do want to challenge their arguments that it's beautiful over there and so ugly and dark over here. Also, have your higher-up point out the benefits of staying with your organization, and the benefits to the employee's career and future.

Most importantly, you want to make sure that you solve the employee's problem. The pitch is all well and good, but, ultimately, you've actually got to do something to solve the employee's problem. This employee has decided to quit working for you, and this is a potential high performer, so they've probably got a valid reason for wanting to leave. It's important to come to the table with a few options for fixing the issues that the employee has presented.

Once you have presented your offer, and made it as enticing as possible, you can ask your employee for a final decision. Hopefully, your employee is feeling comfortable, valued, and esteemed by the end of this meeting—all of which makes a YES response more likely. However, sometimes roadblocks still exist: A spouse or partner who is leaning the other direction, or an aggressive organization heavily recruiting your employee.

Step 3: Confronting Roadblocks

Spouses and partners can have agendas of their own. The best way to deal with them is by speaking to them directly. Many times an employee will say something like, "Well, I'm really considering staying, but my wife is sold on the idea of this new job with CeeCorp." The best way for a manager to respond is to say something like, "Maybe I can talk to her and try to understand why she likes CeeCorp so much, and let her know what we have to offer here." In order to keep the best employees, sometimes managers need to sell significant others on the idea of staying as much as they need to sell employees on staying. If this is the case, then you need to spend some time talking to this person, addressing their concerns, and making your offer clear to them as well.

As far as the competing organization goes, you've got to eliminate them. If they have attempted to steal away your best before, you can bet they will try to do it again. When your employee makes the decision to stay with you, the next step is to give the employee a very formal script to use for declining the offer with this other organization. Ideally, you should be in the room while they're making the call. However, you should do what feels best for the employee. Oftentimes, employees will feel comfortable making the call with you present. It's moral support for them.

The script should be along the lines of, "CeeCorp, I know this will be a disappointment to you, but I won't be accepting your job offer. I'm going to stay here at ABusiness. After talking with several senior executives, it's clear to me I had made a mistake in thinking about leaving. This has nothing to do with money or counteroffers, this is just about what's best for me and my career. My decision is final."

The goal of this call is two-fold. First, you want to shut down that competitor and make sure they don't think about coming back and poaching your employees. Second, you want to make the employee's decision final, psychologically and verbally.

In sum, it is important to fight for your employees. Organizations that take the time to listen to employees that want to leave, and genuinely attempt to fix things in order to keep them, retain up to 50% more employees than organizations that just let them leave.

Putting It Together

Let's return to our opening example with Jake, our carpenter who wants to quit. Jake solemnly approaches you at the end of the day on Friday to give you his two weeks notice. What do you do?

Imagine it goes like this. Jake approaches, gives his speech and you say, "Wow, Jake, I must say, this is quite a surprise. I really want to talk this through with you. Give me five minutes and we'll meet in the trailer to talk about it."

Five minutes later you sit down in the trailer with him and ask, "I really want to know about what led to this decision so that I can understand it fully."

Jake responds, "Well, a few weeks ago the Construction Supervisor at Urbana General Contracting called me and said that he had seen my work at the Historic Home Show. He said they really liked my work and wanted me to come on board and design cabinetry for their retail construction division."

To which you reply, "Hmmmm. I didn't realize you were interested in focusing on cabinetry."

And Jake says, "Well, I don't want to just do cabinetry, but they offered me a really good salary."

You think it over and say, "Must be good. Can I ask what they offered?"

And Jake says, "$5 an hour more than I am making now."

You nod in agreement and ask "There must have been some other things about the job that interested you."

Jake replies, "I really like creating the designs, I think it will be pretty interesting."

You say, "You have a great eye, I can see why that job would grab you. I guess you don't feel like you get to do much of that here."

He says, "Not really. I definitely get to do a variety of carpentry here, which is cool, but I'm usually not the one designing it.

You respond, "Were there other things you wanted to do here, but couldn't?"

"Not really. I mean, I really like working for you, and the guys here are great. It's really a lot of fun. It's mostly that Urbana is a big company and I think I can make more money there and probably get a promotion."

And the talk goes on for a while... Finally, you say "Jake, I think you are a really great carpenter, and I really like working with you. That is why I really want to take some time and think about what you just told me. I don't know whether or not we can work something out, but I don't want you to limit your options right now. So I'm asking you to consider keeping this quiet until Monday. Then let's meet at my office at 9:00 a.m. and we can discuss it some more."

Jake agrees and you, as the owner and president of the company, have some hard thinking to do. You call up your site Foreman and run some ideas past him. You agree to bring him in for the next meeting too.

You all sit down in your office for the Monday morning meeting and you say, "Jake, I've had a rough weekend. I've really thought about everything you've told me. I think you are a fantastic carpenter, as does the Foreman, and we really hope you will choose to stay here. Although we are a small company, I think we have some great opportunities for you. The great thing about working here is the variety of projects and the family attitude. We'd like to offer you more choice about which projects you take. We think you are very talented and very versatile and would be glad to have you on the projects of your choosing. At Urbana, you'd really be doing the same type of designs and projects all the time, which might get boring for a creative person like you. Second, you do have a very good eye. We'd like to really see what you can do, and start you off on designing. I think the rest of the crew would really be behind that; they respect you and the work you've done. I think another great thing about working here is that we all really work together well. I'm not sure you'll find that at a big place like Urbana, where most of the laborers are per diem and come and go. I know they've offered you some good weekly money. I can't really do that. But what I can offer you is a bonus after each project that we finish..."

Jake is feeling good about his potential at the company and decides to stay. With your coaching, he is able to tell Urbana that he is not accepting their offer. He also calls home to tell his wife, who is happy that he is staying with your company, because she knows everyone there and feels like Jake is really well-respected. You were successful. How did you do it? You slowed him down, made your offer, and confronted any roadblocks that prevented you from keeping your best carpenter.

Quiz: Are You Committing Deadly Sin #4?

Directions: Read each of the following statements. If a statement sounds like something you do or would do, or if you agree with it, circle True. If a statement does not sound like something you do or would do, or if you do not agree with it, circle False.

1. When one of my employees quits, it seems to be out of the blue.	*True False*
2. I've been known to just let people leave without a fight.	*True False*
3. I usually don't meet with my employee right away after they tell me they want to quit.	*True False*
4. You shouldn't talk to an employee about the downside of moving to a new company, because they will feel coerced.	*True False*
5. If an employee has decided to quit, they're as good as gone.	*True False*

Scoring: Give yourself 1 point for each True response and 0 points for each False response.

Interpreting Your Score
0 = You are not committing Deadly Sin #4
1 – 2 = You are in danger of committing Deadly Sin #4
3 – 5 = You are committing Deadly Sin #4

DEADLY SIN #5: TURNING YOUR BACK

Cathy was a great Social Worker. Her clients respected her, the staff looked up to her, she did more than her share of work and she was a very pleasant person. But despite everything you did to try to keep her, she really wanted to go into private practice. How do you feel towards Cathy? What do you do now?

Maybe you feel a bit angry or betrayed. After all, you mentored her all these years, thinking that she'd take over your department after you got promoted to Director. Maybe you feel silly, like you should have left to go into private practice as well. Sure, the temptation is just to break ties with her and be done with it. Or decide that she wasn't as great as you thought and bad-mouth her after she leaves. Is that the best direction to take this? Probably not, because, while it makes us feel better in the short term, it cuts off our opportunities in the long run.

Boomerangs, Clients, and Liaisons

When people leave their company on good terms, they tend to keep that company on their mind. They see it as either a good place to work, a good place to patronize, or a good place to refer to others. When people leave remembering that they generally liked working for your company, they are more likely to return in the future. We call these people *boomerangs*. Boomerangs may come back to you at some point in the future. There are three good reasons to like boomerangs. One, they're up to speed, which makes them quicker to train when they come back. So, somebody who quits you, and two years later comes back, is up to speed much faster than a normal new employee. Two, they already understand your values and culture. And three, they bring back new ideas to help you be innovative and keep you from getting stale.

Next, former employees can become future clients. Depending on your industry, they can bring lots of business your way. This is the result of former employees seeing your company as a good place to refer to others. Sometimes ex-employees can be a great source of referrals for potential employees or customers. For example, at Leadership IQ, we have research assistants. Recently, one of our fabulous research assistants left us to go to graduate school. While we were saddened by the loss, we were thrilled that she sent two of her classmates from college to interview for her former position.

Keep It Positive

How do you make the goodbye a "good goodbye" and leave the road open to future relationships? The key is to keep things positive. What we found is that there is a very simple way to end the work relationship but maintain the connection:

1. Throw a Party
2. Touch Base
3. Update

Throwing a goodbye party may sound trite and overly simplistic. But what happens when you throw a party for a valued employee who is leaving? You let them know that they were important and will be missed. It also lets them formally say goodbye to all of their colleagues. The key is to keep the party simple. Another positive result of the party is that it lets the employee leave feeling connected to their coworkers and cements the homey atmosphere of your corporation. Sometimes when employees leave and then start at another company, they are shocked at the lack of fanfare that greets them at the new workplace. They go from knowing everyone and feeling comfortable, to knowing no one and feeling lonely. This lack of fanfare contrasted with the goodbye party can sometimes shock employees into boomeranging back to you fairly quickly.

Second, it is important to give your former employee a call or an e-mail to touch base 30 to 60 days after they leave.

The goal is to "touch base" and see how they are doing in their new job. This keeps the connection going by placing you on their minds at a time when they have so much new information to remember. Finally, you should provide occasional updates about job openings, new programs, etc. You never know when you can get them to boomerang back or refer someone to you.

Gather Data

Whenever an employee leaves, it is important to find out their final reasons for ending the work relationship and their feelings about your organization. While it is easy to simply say goodbye and cut the ties, it is more beneficial to you and your organization to have a formal exit interview to gather data. The reasons for the exit interview are twofold. First, you need to figure out what, if anything, could be fixed to lure this employee back. Second, you need to diagnose and fix any problems that could push other employees away and lead them to quit also.

The exercise of conducting the exit interview does little, in and of itself, to bring employees back. It is the data gathered during the interview that is of use. Unfortunately, many companies don't look at or use the information gathered in these sessions. When Leadership IQ polled companies about their use of exit interviews, approximately 95% said they conduct them, but only 42% said they actually do anything based on the results. Many of them said that they weren't sure what questions they needed to ask, and also that they didn't know who should get the results.

First and foremost, exit interviews should be done after the employee has formally left his or her position, and second, the interview should be conducted by someone besides the employee's former manager. After an employee is a bit settled into their new job, they are less likely to feel coerced and more likely to give honest feedback. At that point, they have no formal ties to your organization and thus, nothing to lose. Ideally, an outside consultant or an HR professional or somebody from an entirely separate part of the organization should conduct the interview. A study by two researchers, Joseph Zarandona and Michael Camuso, compared exit interviews done internally versus exit interviews done externally. What they found was that when employees were interviewed by their manager, 38% said they left for money reasons, but when they were asked by a third party outside researcher only 12% said money was the issue. When they were asked by managers whether poor supervision an issue, only 4% said yes. When they were asked the same question by a third party, 24% agreed that poor supervision was the issue. This study highlights the importance of having an interviewer with as many degrees of separation from the employee as possible. If you want accurate and honest information, you need a neutral third party.

It is important to ask the old standby questions: "What made you leave? Did you share this with your manager? What did you like most? What did you like least? Would you consider returning to the organization?" And it is even more important to ask follow-up questions to each of the responses that an employee gives. Interviewers need to be skilled data gatherers who take the job seriously, and know that the goal is to uncover the *real* reasons employees leave an organization. They need to know that their goal is to find the problems so that others can fix them. Interviewers need to be thorough.

Finally, the question is, "Where should the data go?" And, the response is, to everyone who manages or leads people in the organization. Every manager should know why their employees left, and every leader, including the CEO, should look at the overall results to see if there are problems endemic to the organization or particular departments.

Will the "Quitting Virus" Spread?

One of the most common questions we get about employees who quit is whether they'll make all your other employees want to quit. Here's our answer: One of the biggest reasons for conducting Shoves & Tugs conversations at least every quarter, and preferably every month, is that you'll already know if any other employees are thinking about quitting. The only way for you to find out is to ask, and if you follow the script we gave you previously, you'll be in great shape. Additionally, if you conduct regular Shoves & Tugs conversations, you can ask your employees what they're thinking without looking panicked that someone just quit. This will just be part of your normal monthly Shoves & Tugs conversation.

If the employee that quit is assuming a managerial role and you're worried that they might try to steal away your best employees, here's a great technique: Mentor them. If this is their first management job, tell them how excited you are that they have this opportunity to create a brand-new team without having to tackle the emotional baggage that comes from managing former peers. This will make them seriously reconsider taking anyone.

Then, regardless of their previous management experience, ask how you can help them. Be there for them. Serve as a mentor. You want to do this for two reasons: First, you'll make them feel guilty if they consider stealing your people away (and it's often just enough to dissuade them). Second, do you know the old saying "keep your friends close and your enemies closer?" Well, the more you keep in contact with them, the more likely you are to glean some insight into their next steps. And that may be just the competitive intelligence you need to stay one step ahead of them.

The bottom line is that regardless of how betrayed you feel, and how much you want revenge, you can't really do anything to punish quitting employees. And if you try to do something retaliatory, you'll only make yourself look petty and mean-spirited. We've all had the occasional "Tony So-

prano for a day" fantasy, but the smartest move after someone quits is to keep your cool, keep as close to the quitting
employee as possible, and keep as close to your remaining
employees as possible.

And remember, "dissing" the departed employee to your
remaining employees is unlikely to guilt them into staying
(that's not how guilt works). Instead, what will happen is
that when they do feel like quitting, they'll be too scared to
tell you.

Putting It Together

Cathy was a great Social Worker. While you feel badly about
her leaving, you want to keep the relationship with her going.
On her last day of work, you and your staff throw her a
lovely goodbye luncheon in the staff lounge. Everyone has
pitched in to make homemade treats, and at the end of the
party, you present her with a personalized clipboard as a
goodbye gift from you and the staff. Cathy says a tearful
farewell, and promises to keep in touch.

Two weeks later, an associate from Human Resource has an
exit interview with Cathy. He discovers that, while Cathy
had planned on eventually going into private practice, she
was having some conflicts with one of her colleagues that
hastened her departure. Still, Cathy left feeling positive
about her work at your agency and her relationship with you.

One month down the road, you pick up the phone to give Cathy a call and see how she is doing. She is not available, but you leave her a nice voicemail message letting her know that you are thinking of her and hoping that her practice is taking off. Later that day you see that she left you an e-mail saying that she was pleasantly surprised by your message and that she hopes to reach you soon because she wants to refer a client to your agency.

Who knows what will happen further down the road. Maybe Cathy will return to work for you someday. Or maybe she will simply send more clients your way. But, whatever happens, the relationship is there because you didn't turn your back.

Quiz: Are You Committing Deadly Sin #5?

Directions: Read each of the following statements. If a statement sounds like something you do or would do, or if you agree with it, circle True. If a statement does not sound like something you do or would do, or if you do not agree with it, circle False.

1. I don't talk to my ex-employees anymore.	*True* *False*
2. We don't do "goodbye parties" for employees who quit.	*True* *False*
3. Employees who quit on me are very aware that I'm angry at them.	*True* *False*
4. I do the exit interview myself.	*True* *False*
5. We don't hear from our employees once they have left.	*True* *False*

Scoring: Give yourself 1 point for each True response and 0 points for each False response.

Interpreting Your Score
0 = You are not committing Deadly Sin #5
1 – 2 = You are in danger of committing Deadly Sin #5
3 – 5 = You are committing Deadly Sin #5

CONCLUSION:
TAKE THE FIRST STEP

Imagine you're the CEO of a large hospital. You're facing staffing shortages in your most important roles (like nurses and pharmacists), a new study shows that nursing vacancies can contribute to patient deaths, your overall turnover number is horrible, the board is breathing down your neck, a nurses union is trying to organize your hospital, and if you don't act fast you could lose your job.

Imagine you're the Assistant Manager for a large discount store called SaveADollarMart. You've got 80 direct reports, they all make minimum wage (or slightly over), turnover exceeds 100%, you've got lots of seasonal workers, and you can't name more than 30 of your employees.

Don't Try to Save the World

The Core (2003) is a highly entertaining disaster film (we're leadership experts, not film critics, so take our review with a grain of salt). In the film, the Earth's core stops rotating and our planet's magnetic sheath collapses, meaning the planet is about to be destroyed. So a manned mission is dispatched to the center of the Earth to "jumpstart" the planet. Among the heroes dispatched to save the earth are Dr. Josh Keyes (an Indiana Jones-like geophysicist who ultimately saves the planet) and his best friend Dr. Serge Leveque (a French atomic weapons expert, husband, and father of 2 little girls). After the death of their first crewmember, Dr. Keyes becomes overwhelmed by the prospect of trying to save everyone on the planet from certain death. To Serge he says "My God, the whole thing just feels so overwhelming. Do we really have a chance?" Serge knowingly pats his friend on the shoulder and says "Josh my friend, nobody can save the world. It's just too much. You are trying to save 6 billion lives. I am just trying to save 3 lives; my wife and daughters. That's all I can comprehend. That's all I can do. But I can do that."

Here's our advice to executives and managers: Don't try to save 6 billion people, just try to save three. If you try to save the world, your brain will overload. It's just too much. Just find a few people you can save, and put your energy there.

There's a dirty little secret about large-scale retention initiatives: they oversell and underdeliver. Hundreds of thousands of dollars get spent, and the results are underwhelming. Every so often an organization will claim success from a large-scale initiative, but you'll usually find that the whole organization didn't improve, just a few managers did. And that's the point.

To improve retention, you've got to act locally, at the individual level. Even if you're the CEO of a Fortune 100 company, improving retention is a local initiative. Let's imagine you're the CEO of an organization with 10,000 employees. With a typical 10:1 span of control, you've probably got 1,000 leaders. And let's say that around 40% of the workforce is a top priority for your retention efforts (i.e. 4,000 employees are high performers and/or in hard-to-replace roles). So 1,000 managers have to focus on retaining 4,000 employees. For people that hate to do math in their heads, every manager has to retain 4 people. (Would you like to retain 80% of the workforce? Of course. But as we discussed earlier, you've got to start with the critical people and positions.)

When we tell executives that they need to retain their most critical 4,000 employees, they get a bit panicky. And as you might expect, the initial reaction is to create a major initiative to transform retention practices. But when we tell them that every manager has to retain their 4 most critical people, the task doesn't seem so daunting.

"Many hands make light work" goes the saying. And nowhere is that more true than in retention efforts. Jim Collins made the same discovery in his landmark book *Good to Great*. If every leader does a little bit, the wheel starts turning, a few successes turn into hundreds and thousands of successes, and the whole organization starts to see extraordinary results.

What follows are the practical first steps to help you and your organization get the wheel turning.

First Steps for CEOs and Executives

For senior executives the first step is simple: Train every manager how to retain a few of their most critical people. Most leaders commit at least a few of the deadly sins outlined in this book. So give every leader a day of training on how to implement the practices in this book. Before you spend hundreds of thousands of dollars on a major initiative, invest in a day of training. It's much less expensive and exponentially more effective.

Once you've trained every leader, you must mandate five things. Of course, we want every leader to implement all the tactics outlined in this book. But if you implement the following five tactics within 90 days of the training, you'll be off to a great start. You'll start to see your employee retention improve, and then you can get to work on everything else.

1. Every leader must create a Retention Priority Grid for their direct reports (see Deadly Sin #1). These grids must be discussed with, and approved by, each leader's immediate supervisor (all the way up to the CEO).

2. Every leader must conduct Shoes & Tugs conversations with each of their top retention priorities. A summary of each conversation (see Deadly Sin #2) must be discussed with, and approved by, each

leader's immediate supervisor (all the way up to the CEO).

3. Change the initiation process for new hires (see Deadly Sin #3). We suggest requiring that a welcome card be sent to every new hire's home before they start, mandating a buddy system, and directing new hires to their new manager before they begin their orientation.

4. Every new hire must be personally welcomed by at least one senior executive within their first 2 days.

5. Every leader must analyze the results of all their Shoves & Tugs conversations, as well as their exit interview data, and find one opportunity for self-improvement. Leaders should look for a common complaint or a frequently cited demotivator, etc. Even the greatest leaders can improve (remember that Tiger Woods has a coach) and this is a fantastic opportunity to deepen your leadership talent pool.

First Steps for Managers and Supervisors

For managers and supervisors, the first steps are similar to the ones for senior executives, with one very important addition (the Manager-For-A-Day program).

1. Create a Retention Priority Grid for your direct reports (see Deadly Sin #1).

2. Conduct Shoes & Tugs conversations with each of your top retention priorities (see Deadly Sin #2).

3. Change the initiation process for new hires (see Deadly Sin #3). Send a welcome card to every new hire's home before they start, find some volunteers for a buddy system, and meet with your new hires before they begin their orientation.

4. Analyze your Shoes & Tugs conversations, as well as your exit interview data, and find one opportunity for self-improvement.

5. Create a Manager-For-A-Day program. Take your 3-5 top performers and invite them to spend one day a week working alongside you in a managerial capacity. Give them a mix of both the mundane and the interesting aspects of management. Present it as an opportunity to do some different and potentially interesting work, but don't oversell it—let the work speak for itself. And if you have to delegate some of their current work, just do it. There are three reasons to implement this program. First, you get some 1:1 time with your most important people and you'll build a stronger bond. Second, you get some extra help. If you've got 80 direct reports, you can't interact with everyone. But if you've got five additional

high performers serving as part-time managers under your direction, you can cover a lot more ground. Third, this is a chance for you to evaluate potential leaders, and give them the chance to see if they enjoy managerial work. The Manager-For-A-Day program is one of the most successful tactics we've seen. And as an added bonus, this will do more to prevent managerial burnout than just about anything else.

Conclusion

This book was designed to be easy to read and easy to implement. There are a few key mistakes that virtually every leader in every organization makes, and these mistakes (aka deadly sins) undermine our retention efforts. But if you take the necessary steps to correct and eliminate the deadly sins, you'll leave your competition in the dust.

We've seen organizations correct the deadly sins in under 30 days and radically transform their ability to retain employees. Correcting the deadly sins doesn't require a major initiative involving large budgets and an army of consultants. Correcting the deadly sins requires an understanding of the problem and the disciplined execution of the solution.

REFERENCES

Collins, J. *Good to Great* (New York: HarperCollins, 2001).

Doebbeling, BN et al. "Comparative Efficacy of Alternative Handwashing Techniques on Nosocomial Infections in Intensive Care Units." *New England Journal of Medicine*, 1992.

Goldman, D. and Larson, E. "Hand Washing and Nosocomial Infection." *New England Journal of Medicine*, 1992.

Haley, RW; Culver, DH; Morgan, WM; Emori, TG; Munn, VP; and Hooton, TP. "The Efficacy of Infection Control Programs in Preventing Nosocomial Infection in U.S. Hospitals." *American Journal of Epidemiology*, 1985.

Kohn, LT; Corringan, JM and Donaldson, MS (eds). *To Err is Human: Building a Safer Health System*, (National Academies Press, 1999).

Meade, PS et al. "Food Related Illness and Death in the United States." *Emerging Infectious Diseases*, 1999.

Michaels, E.; Handfield-Jones, H and Axelrod, B. *The War for Talent*. (McKinsey & Company, 2001).

Zarandona, JL and Camuso, MA. "A Study of Exit Interviews: Does the Last Word Count?" *Personnel*, 1985.

ABOUT THE AUTHORS

MARK MURPHY is the Founder & CEO of Leadership IQ, the world's largest provider of online leadership seminars. Mark's work has appeared in *Business Week*, the *Harvard Management Update*, *USA Today*, *Forbes* and *Executive Excellence*. Mark is also coauthor of the #1 bestseller *Leading on the Edge of Chaos* (Prentice Hall, 2002). He's a 3-time nominee for *Modern Healthcare's* "Most Powerful People in Healthcare Award" joining a list of luminaries including President George W. Bush, Senator Bill Frist, and Senator Hillary Clinton. Mark has lectured at Yale University, the University of Rochester, the University of Miami and Tufts University, and has been the featured speaker for hundreds of groups. His clients have included DuPont, HP and the Surgeon General.

ANDREA BURGIO-MURPHY, PH.D. is Executive Vice President of Leadership IQ. A well-known clinical psychologist, Dr. Murphy also serves as adjunct faculty at George Washington University and serves on the Board of Directors of the Capitol Area Crisis Response Team in Washington, DC. She directs Consulting Services for Leadership IQ and has presented to more than a hundred groups in corporate, academic and government settings. Dr. Murphy holds a Ph.D., M.A. and B.A. from the University of Rochester.

ON-SITE TRAINING SESSIONS

The Deadly Sins of Employee Retention is available as a one or two day on-site training program for executives and managers. The program is also available as a keynote presentation. Both of the authors are available for presentations and are consistently the top-rated speakers at national conferences.

Other popular onsite training sessions include:
- The Deadly Sins of Employee Retention
- Executive Team Tune-Up
- The Deadly Sins of Hiring
- The Deadly Sins of Teams
- Influence Without Authority
- Improve or Remove: Managing Low Performers
- What Great Managers Do Differently

To engage Leadership IQ for your next conference or in-house event, contact:

Leadership IQ Seminar Services
800-814-7859
www.leadershipiq.com
info@leadershipiq.com

WEBINARS AND CDS

Leadership IQ is the world's largest provider of online leadership seminars. Each 1-hour program combines streaming video, audio and cutting-edge content to create the most unique and engaging training experience available.

Popular 1-hour webinar & CD programs include:

The 5 Deadly Sins of Retention
The 5 Deadly Sins of Hiring
The 5 Deadly Sins of Motivation
The 7 Deadly Sins of Meetings
The 5 Deadly Sins of Time Management
The 5 Deadly Sins of Teams
Managing High Conflict Personalities
Persuasive Presentations
What's Your Emotional IQ?
Getting Individuals to Change
Influence Without Authority
Improve or Remove: Managing Low Performers
Motivating B Players
How to Speak So Others Will Listen
Can't We All Just Get Along?

Visit www.leadershipiq.com to learn more.

Readers of this book get special access to a complimentary Leadership IQ webinar. To view the program visit:

www.leadershipiq.com/rct1234.html